Ice Cream And Suicide

By Jack Ray

"And in this harsh world draw thy breath in pain. To tell my story." -Shakespeare's *Hamlet*

Pandora's Box

How can I ever move on...

No.
I will move on.
I'm finished with
Your games.
You've hurt me
For the last time.

This book is
A testimony to that.
I'll show you
Everything you've lost
Everything you've forgotten
Everything you made me feel
Everything you did to destroy me.
This is us.
This will always be us.
And this is all that's left
Of us.

1201:16

We were cold
    So you asked for hot chocolate
Rather I was told
    That you needed it

Snow fall from heaven
    Lights hang from every inch
The show starts at seven
    Better watch the dance

"You could do that"
    I always tried to encourage
"No, I'm too fat"
    Trust me she isn't at all

Ornaments sparked off the tree
    So we gathered round the center
Didn't really impress me honestly
    But I was focused on her

As we turned away to leave
    I asked about her hot chocolate
She had something up her sleeve
    When she said "It's perfect"

Then as we walked away
    My eyes were glued to her beauty
I asked about her day
    "With you? It's perfect."

~*Why did you lie to me?*

Devout

I told myself I'd stop.
Stop loving the wrong person
And quit giving my life
To a façade who takes
Everything from me.

These are the lies
I'll tell myself.

Secretary Of War

Look at you
Living like what you did
Was nothing but a pinch
When really
It was an atomic bomb.

Free Samples, Take One Please!

I sympathize with those
Who have been given a
Taste of eternity
Just to be told
That it's sold out.

Blue-Ridge Mountains

Her eyes are
The rolling hills and skyline
That tell the history
Of her earth
From creation to obliteration
The moment I marched
Into her forest
Denatured her flora
And enslaved her fauna
Settled in that perfect world
That was not so perfect
After all, thanks to me.
Women like her
With eyes like her
Are meant to be free.
There is no one deserving
Of them and to believe
That you are,
Is a slap in the face
Of Mother Nature.

Masochistic

You know you do this to yourself.
You break your own heart.
Flood your mind with the thoughts.
It's all in how you see yourself.
Only you have the power to stop this.
But I know why you haven't.
Without this, what do you have left?

Back To Square One

I can't say I didn't
See this coming.
When will you learn
To stop being so
Stubborn
And allow me to
Finish what we started.

Priceless Love

You're so precious
With your
Eyes of sapphire
Locks of gold
And heart of ruby.
All too valuable
But no one could
Ever put a price on
Your gorgeous body.

Desire Isn't A Strong Enough Word

There's not a spot
On your body
I want to forget.
The softness of your
Skin in mine.
Every pore is unique,
And yet they all lead
To the heart of
My angel of pleasure.

My Confessional

Truth is I do miss you.
And yes
I do want you.
I want you more than
Anything this
Piece of shit rock
We call Earth could
Ever offer the likes of me.
And there's more too.

The sound you produce
May be the most
Alluring and addictive drug
To hit the market.
I know this, yet I want it.
I want it so badly.
I want to play that drug
On repeat 24/7/365.

And when we encounter each other,
It's like the first time we've ever met.
I'll find myself staring at you
Undressing you in my head,
Revealing those cute curves that

Make up the little frame of the one I love
Because baby,
The truth is I do miss you.
And yes
I do want you.

~Your secret admirer.

Wash, Rinse, Repeat

I am the ink
That stains your clothes
And marks your skin.
Such an anomaly,
This I am certain.

Over Their Heads

You know there's a problem
When someone says
"Don't tell"

...It was fun nonetheless.

The Love That Strangles

comes only from
her. I need her.
the love that strangles.
smothering, suffocating
my cries for help. blinding
in passion to live
again inside her blood.
ignored. forgotten.
a fool to man and
a fool to her.
the love that strangles.
I hear her voice.
a beautiful pitch.
false promises are what
she sings. a melody,
a master, a slave.
an orchestra of
sound. she speaks in
a tongue of deceit
embodied in
beauty. twisted hymns
manipulate even a
saint.
the love that strangles.

when you see her.
cloaked in golden
rays of desolation.
eyes that pierce the
soul of man, blue,
as the talisman of
Nazar. strong, lean,
and inviting. *Delilah.*
the love that strangles
comes only from
her. I need her.
I need her.

Out Of Batteries

I laid into you
To feel your heart
Beat with mine,
What I heard
Was silence.

Sadistic

I cried out for help.
The pain of us
Was numbing over
But in a sick
Twist of fate
The only one I
Could vent to
Was you.
The very person
Who made me this way.

Perceptions

Sometimes I look at her and think,
"Damn, she's otherworldly,
 There's not a single soul out there like her's."
Except mine.

Perceptions II

It's a crazy thing
Thinking you're so close to someone
When really
You're worlds apart.

Perceptions III

You know as well as I do
That the memories
Begin to alter.
They take on personalities
Of their own.
They become self-aware caricatures
Of who we are and what
We want them to be.
Good,
Bad,
Or ugly
Our minds show us what
We believe,
What we felt at the time
Of sanctification.

Heyyyy

The amount of
Self discipline
It takes
To keep me
From texting you
Is absurd.

I Can't Be Alone With You

A relationship
In which both parties
Are afraid to be alone
With each other
Isn't real.

Illimitable Dominion

There's a tremendous
Tragedy in the performance of
Two lovers.
One in which
The brave and the bold
Are ridiculed and denounced
By the lame and the sheepish
Till the brave become cowards
The bold become servants
To the serpent who pulls
All the strings.
And once the tongues
Are tied in a knot
That even the Almighty
Could not untie
The couple will live happily ever after...
Never to be heard of again.

Plan B

Say it with me...
I am strong.
I am good enough.
I will never be
Someone's backup plan.

Green Mushrooms

The hardest part is knowing,
That we've come so far,
That you'd never wanna start over
And give us another chance.

Looks Can Be Deceiving

She's the type of girl
To walk you to the
Edge of the earth,
Spend the afternoon with you
And shove you off afterwards.

Good Mourning

I know you don't know this
But I think you should...

I wake up every morning
To your face, smiling back at me.
It's burned into my skull
Like a phantom longing for
A place to stay.
You follow me no matter
Where I lay my head,
I'll awake and you'll be there.

And it hurts.
It hurts.
It hurts so bad because
I would waste a million lifetimes
Doing nothing but chasing you.
Die day after day, if it meant
Having you to hold again.
I would latch on to that hope of us
Like my world depended on it.
Not just *my world*,
But *your world*.
In this case I would never let go.
I would never let go of your world
Just as you have never let go of mine.
That's why I see you every morning,
I know you haven't forgotten,

And I know you still care.
Deep down...it's there.
Our world.

You Could Stitch A Quilt And Stay Warm

Rip through my heart
Tear it to pieces
Believe me when I say
There's enough love there
To go around.

Gobstopper

People act hard
On the outside
But really are soft
At the core.
You must have gotten
This mixed up along the way.

The Void

My everything
Dances in the center
Of the floor
Surrounded by rays of sunshine
And petals from the most
Exotic and extravagant flowers
Known to sprout their beautiful bodies
To this earth
And yet
No one...

No one dances with her
Because everyone knows
That she moves in a way that
No body can keep up.

Especially not me,
Who watches her in awe
Across the floor
In a void
Loved by no one.

Life In The Cage

Hook me by your tongue
Whisper in my ear that
You love me
Shackle the chain
Around my heel
And tell me that
We'll be happy
Together forever
As you prepare
My collar and muzzle.

The Love That Strangles II

Tenderly touch
And drag me under
The fields of silk and cotton
The heat of you against me
Suffocate me with your heart
And suppress all sound.

We shall speak no evil
Forevermore.

Nostalgic Nightmares

You dream
Of meeting someone
Just like me again,
So you can have all your fun.

Permanent Markers

I never knew how embarrassing
It would be to talk about you now.

This Is An Audio Recording For Your Sanity

Welcome to this weeks
Guided meditation.
Close your eyes.
Stop and listen to your thoughts.
Imagine you're in your happy place.
Imagine this wonderful place
Surrounded by everyone you love
Doing everything you love to do.
...
...
...
Now open your eyes,
And realize that this happy place
Does not exist.

Unrequited

In an ironic way,
It's sort of funny
How we learn to love those
Who never seem
To deserve it.

Red Flags

I'm looking for the answers...
So are you
And if you're looking for help
Go elsewhere
Cause all I've found
In my search
In my youth
Is heartache
The longing for affection
The hole it creates
How you'll end up
Digging
Digging
Digging
But ultimately drown
In your own attempts
At life after love
You'll drown
Looking for the answers
So go elsewhere.

There's No Cure

Unlike her love,
Her demons are contagious.

Your Apologies Are Unapologetic And Untimely

God, I hope someday
Someone makes you
Feel just like me.
Alone.
Then you can apologize.

The Good Samaritan

I'm slaving away
At the pages
Just to warn the others
About your transgressions.

Nothing's Good Enough For My Girl

I could give you the Sun
        Then you'd ask for the moon
I would steal you the moon
        Just to beg for the stars
Once I hand you the stars
        You would look up above
See nothing up high
        In the black midnight sky
Look me dead in the eye
        And demand the Earth.

The Love That Strangles III

Oh the things I would do
To be with you
Are ruthless and cold
But daring and bold
I'd fight every villain
I'd slay every monster
I'd stand up to darkness
And strangle the heartless.
But truth be told
I'd follow blindfold
And show those that taint gold
The end as foretold.

This Is Not Rhetorical

Are you competing
With the Devil
To see who can
Collect the most souls?

I'm sure you're winning by a landslide.

Sincerely Your Truly Beloved

I can't go anywhere anymore.
I can't leave my bedroom.
Because you cursed me
Ruined everything that I could ever
Experience with another woman.
You've taken it all from me and
Left me with nothing to my name.
Now all I ever see in their faces
As they walk by is you.

~Thank you.

Nothing Helps You Grow Faster Than Suffering

The way I wrote about you before...
If you could see me now.

Happy Birthday!

Sixteen.
You can take on
The world
And everyone in it.

Seventeen.
The world
Shows you what
It has too offer.

Eighteen.
The realization
That the world
Is a horrible place
Full of suffering
And no one is
Prepared for it's
Show and tell.

Stay Determined

Keep pushing forward,
So one day you can take
A look behind you
See all the ones
Who've ever wronged you
And scream
"Fuck you too."

Prayer Of Undoing

Twisting and turning into me
From beyond
The valves of my heart leak
Tears from a blonde
If I were to perish before I awake
I pray thee O'Lord, her soul do forsake.

East Of Eden

She'd kill family
As long as she had
Something to gain
Or something to prove.

Self-Contained

You're quiet.
Self-contained.
I like that about you.
The way you hide
Your gorgeous eyes
By looking at the ground
Because you're afraid.
Afraid of the judgement
That people often pass
On and on and on.
But I wouldn't worry.

No.
You don't need them
Because you know yourself.
Others may act tough
But they don't know you
Like you know you.
All you fought for.
All you believe in.
It looks good on you.
Don't be afraid to show the world
What it's missing.

Rigged Machines

To be hurt so badly, so often
By the one
You'd trade your life to save.

1.8 Million Years Ago

You are promising
Like snowfall in winter.
Cool.
Calm.
Beautiful.
Unique.

Have You Heard Of The Ugly Duckling?

One day you're gonna see,
The biggest mistake you ever made
Was thinking I was good for nothing.

Talk In The Next Lifetime?

Hey, it's me.
Yeah, crazy right? I know it's been awhile.
How have you been?
That's good, I've been alright.
Yeah classes are tough but it'll work itself out.
Is that right? Well that's great!
I always knew how smart you were.
You haven't changed too much have you?
Still love hanging out at the football games?
You still perform? I'd love to go see you sometime.
You know I miss you.
No, I really do. We had a lot of good times!
…
Maybe we could go for that drive we talked about.
Catch up, you know?
…
Yeah, I know. Well I was just checking up on you.
The drive was a long shot I know.
Yeah, you're probably right.
It's just that...
Ok yeah well you know how it is.
How we are.
That's who we choose to be.
I'm sorry this is my fault.

No you're fine, I really missed you that's all.
I don't know what I was thinking.
It's just that...

...goodbye.

(It's just that I've changed I swear)

Ice Cream And Suicide

You'll strike me down
With your words
But never deal
The final blow...
You leave that to me.

How inhumane.

Latrodectus

This elegant dance we share
You, then me, then you again
Until one of us gets caught.
It's something out of
The hunter in you,
The prey in me.
The next part never ceases
To amaze me.
The way you turn a kiss
Into a kill.

BFF

The wall you built
Between us is both
Impenetrable and nonexistent.

Like Baking A Cake
(With Extra Sprinkles On Top)

Everything about you
Makes me believe
God poured a little too
Much flawless in
When he made you.

Don't Forget To Leave A Tip

There's not much difference
Between fire and ice.
Both share the same hue of yellow with gold.
Both lean and selfish to the user.
They each deliver death through burns,
And the lucky survivors might even
scar for a lifetime.
I could only imagine the agony of it all.

Yet both are essential to our life.
And of course by that I mean
They give us choice of
How we want our coffee to be served.
Hot or iced, yet still one and the same.
You're gonna get your coffee either way
And Lord knows
That coffee's gonna kill you.

Pros And Cons

You are the most
Gorgeous woman I've
Ever laid eyes on.
But you're also
The weakest.

Under The Floorboards

My room is a crypt,
A flood of demons
Lurks around every corner
And monsters live under my bed.
The same bed we called home.
You left them with your soul.

Views From My Dorm Room

Out of sight out of mind
Isn't always the case.
I can feel you pulling and
Tugging from miles away.
Every night's the same
And I still feel this pain.
God only knows what
I'd do to get you out of
My head and into my bed.

Robin

I guess it's one of those nights where
I wish I could check up on you so
I could feel myself falling in love again.

Peanut Butter And Jelly

Think about what
We were going to become
And try not to cry
When you realize you threw away
The only thing in your life that was
Perfect.

Everyday At Six

I saw you again last night.
We were so happy together
Nothing like watching the
Ocean's waves crash into
A lovers' paradise.
Just me and you.
Just us, with only the moon
As our guide.
You kissed me and said
"Hold me tight and don't ever
Let go of the love between us."
Then I heard my alarm clock.

Where's The Spark?

I have to leave you.
I'm sorry, but I have to.
You have always been
There for me and for that
I owe you the world...
But even the world isn't
Big enough for me and her.
I understand that she too
Is a friend of yours...
That's why I'm leaving you all to
Live the life we dreamed up in
Our prepubescent minds.
The kingdom we built.
I'll never know why she and I
Decided to play with fire.
I guess I'm never meant to know.
What I do know is that without me
Constantly drawn to the
Natural aura of her beauty,
You will have so much
Happiness ahead.
I also know that seeing
Her life in the presence
Of another man...

It would kill me,
In fact maybe the
Thought itself did kill me.
Maybe that's why
I'm no longer here.
You knew as well as
I did that one of us was
Going to get burned.
We couldn't share
Your friendship
And it's simple.

I chose to vanish because
It's easier to save the life
Of another, than to
Pick up the pieces
Of your own.

That's Gonna Get Infected

If I had the choice
Of hearing your name
Or walking on glass,
I'd take the glass every time
Cause I know there's no difference
Besides the clean up,
Which isn't as bloody.

Thrill Of The Kill

I am not controlled
By my thoughts.
Nor am I controlled
By my emotions.
I'm controlled by
An ignorant dictator
Who leads me
To devastation
And to commit actions
I know are morally unjust.
This is simply
Her way of having fun.
Using me to wage a war
On herself.

Nothing Is Easy

Tough love is a wild ride
And it does no good for either side.

So I Prayed For You...

I dream about your love,
Does it come from up above?
Your eyes of ocean blue,
Show me visions of something new.
Your hair shines holy light,
If only for the night.
Your voice takes me far away,
To places I wish to stay.
Give me one chance to prove,
And I swear I'll make the move.
To be your one and only,
Leave me no longer lonely.
I think we're perfect for each other,
Let us love one another.

1 John 2:15

Everyone I see
Looks like you.
Does that mean I'm in love with the world?
No, just the opposite.

Maybe You Need To Slay More Monsters

I've been staring into the Abyss,
She hasn't once looked back.

Maybe You Need To Slay More Lives

I think the worst thing
About becoming a monster
Is not knowing
That's what you are
Until it's too late.

Friends Of Friends Are Just Friends

I know her.
She knows me.
We're more than just friends
In this twisted fantasy

Without him here
No one will know
Without him here
No one will know

She holds me tight
But I hold tighter
I know it's not right
But I'm no fighter

Too quick to give in
To this evil desire
Forgive me my sin
I sparked the fire

The passion consumes
And it burns even brighter
Don't tell the groom
As I said I'm no fighter

Now every night
My sweet lover confesses
"I know it's not right,
But we'll hide the messes"

"I know it's not right"
My sweet lover confesses
But it's only a dream,
Yes it's only a dream
Thank God.

Overwrite Previous

Now that you left me,
Are you happier
Knowing that no
One could ever
Love you like I did.

Globe 1599

Here you are again
On the center stage
Of my thoughts.
That's where you belong,
You always were good at acting.

Dear Sister

Pins and needles doesn't even remotely describe
The way those words echo through my head.
The feeling's more industrial, nails and screws.

Practice Makes Perfect (Mask On)

You kissed me
You didn't want to
But you did it
Again
And again
And again
And again.

I told you I loved you
You didn't want to
But you said it back
Again
And again
And again
And again
And again.

Traumatic Stress Disorder

Remind me
Of bad memories
That have yet
To transpire.

Trophy Hunter

You made me your fool.
Showed off your slave to everyone.
Ruined my reputation.
But what's a reputation
To a doormat.

Life Of Dog

It's sad to think
That all the time we
Spent together
I now spend sitting
Here alone in the dark
Waiting for the answer
To my compelling question
Which we both know
Has no solution.

Pumpkin Spice Lattes

Every time I saw you cry,
Every time I saw you smile,
Every time ended in me buying you coffee.

Black Holes And Black Hearts

I write from the heart
Whatever's left of it.
Ooze leaks from my veins
And thickens the arteries.
It helps my blood stain black.
Perfect for a bedside poem
Or regularly scheduled nightmare,
Ink bloats from my thoughts
Are nothing but hallucinations,
Visions of the past
The past that went up in flames.
All that's left is the ash and char
Of my tainted memories of you.
It helps my blood stain black.
And the taste that you left in me
Turned my salvia to tar and asphalt.
Now every time I open my mouth
Chunks of lies and abuse hit the floor.
It helps my blood stain black.

Boundless

"I'd go to the ends of the earth to be with you."

~Huh, seems a little limited don't you think?

Testing One-Two

Look at yourself in the mirror.
Who are you?
Nobody.
No, you're worse.
You're somebody without a purpose.

Meiosis

We went our separate ways a long time ago.
Told each other to never look back at
What had been...or could've been.
Unbeknown to you, I relive that moment everyday.

Just Get Over It Already!

Oh God,
What have I done
To deserve this torment.
Release these feelings
From me O'Lord
And fill the hole that remains.
The acid inside burns away
All sense I have left.
It sticks to my bones
And rattles my heart
Until it would leave me physically ill.
All the while she beckons me to
Crawl back to hell,
Where I have been misguided
Into believing that here
Is where I'll find my love.

Silver Bells

That night we were cold
And snow was falling all around us
But my love for you
Came in a gift.
It was enough to keep us both warm.

Versailles

Love is nothing
But two sides
Going to war
Over the same thing

Not everyone survives.

Half The Man

A tree without it's bark
     A fire without a spark
A room without it's walls
     A bird without it's calls
A ball that isn't round
     A song without a sound
A cloud without a sky
     You without an alibi
This is how it feels
     To kiss at your heels
Left me all alone
     A dog without a bone.

Mahakali

Another morning, another slit
Let the blood drip slowly down the drain
Flowing away from my unattainable desires
Into a sewer
Where my past lives on in bountiful love.
I hope my offering tastes sweet.
Because I've given up more than I can handle.

Famous Last Words

Please, just figure it out already.

Queen's Gambit

If you can learn
One thing from a game
Of Chess, it's that
The easiest way to
End the life of a king
Is through a queen.

There's something in that.

The Innocence Of Childhood

Me and you,
Sitting in a tree.
K-I-S-S-I-N-G
First comes love,
Then comes marriage,
Then comes you saying
"I think we need to see other people."

Guardian Angel

It's Friday night
You're all alone
You look for parties
On your phone
One down Main Street
Two Downtown
If you're lucky
You'll hear the sound
Of the music blaring
And know it's the one
To spend your evening
Having all the fun

Drink and drink
Then drink some more
Till no more drinks
Can be drank anymore
Then when you're tired
And feeling blue
He'll be by your side
To comfort you
He'll hand you a drink
To stay relaxed
Then before you know it

He'll put on his mask

His intentions seem good
You believe he's true
But deep down inside
He's here only for you

As you return home
You'll never be the same
The man took from you
And you think you're to blame
I knew it was wrong
A bad idea of course
To go out on the town
As Beauty's purest source
And I worried for you
Since when I first heard
But I couldn't stop you
You trashed me to the curb.

Grains Of Sand

Love is when
A minute together
Feels like an hour
And a day
A lifetime.

Chronos' Pendant

As time ticks by
I know you'll forget about me,
But I'll never forget about you.

Through Thick And Thin

She's left you for good
But even now without her
You're unhappy.
Do you even know
What you want?
She's left you for good
To find a man
That will show her
Joy and fortune
None of which
You have ever offered to her.
She's left you for good
Because you've been
To much of a burden,
A mosaic of broken pieces
That requires constant
Love and attention.
She's left you for good
And is never coming back.

3,500 People Unintentionally Drown Every Year

If you were the water and I the boat,
Would we sink or stay afloat?
You'd likely snatch me down,
Laugh and watch me drown.
Then send me to the floor,
Where I'd stay forevermore.
With everything I'd leave behind,
There'd be one thing on my mind.
If you were the water and I the boat,
Would we sink or stay afloat?

CTRL+ALT+DEL

Don't stop by if you aren't gonna stay.

The Honeymoon Stage

I tried to fight this feeling.
This feeling that is more like a
Horror coming over me.
I held it back for so long,
But ten thousand years
Of constant awareness
Makes a man sore and fatigued.
War and ruin all for nothing
But the grace of a new day.
These days are over,
Dawn has broke up the sky
Into shards of heart and lead.
The Pestilence finally scaled my
Fortress walls and contorted
The tongues of my men to speak.
It spoke words I had always
Sworn never to utter:

"I wish I had never met you."

Hello, My Name Is Us

Statistically you're bound to find a partner.
Well that's what they tell us,
Those of us who've managed to find everyone
Except someone to love.
In most cases, someone to love us back.
The reality is there are no guarantees in life,
Statistics or not,
And that some of us are just gonna die alone.

Messages I Wish I Could Send

I miss you.
I do, I promise.

Burden 2 Bare

I find it quite entertaining
You think there's love remaining
But love is simply black and white
And deep down you know I'm right

There's nothing left so sit and sigh
Stay in bed and wait to die
There's nothing left accept your fate
You think you love, but I know you hate.

Irregular Heartbeat

Dot dot
Slash
Dot dash
Dot dot
Space
Dash dash dash
Space
Dot dot
Dot dash
Space
Dot
Slash
Dash dot
Dash dash
Space
Dash dash dash
Space
Dot dot
Dash

Only you could make the words
'I love you' so complicated.

Goldilocks And The Three Bears

Live with you?
Live without you?
These are the troubles that plague mankind.

Fresh Paint

Left me devoted to your love
While you weighed our probability.
All the times we never shared
Because you just think too much.

Lotus Petals

No one understands
How easy it is to
Confuse wildflowers
With tongues of flame.

Home Is Where The Heart Is

I prayed to God
For you to come
Into my life.
You did.
You fucked it up.
But here I lie
Praying to God
For you to come back.

Try Shaking It More

It's painful
Seeing pictures of you
Knowing I'm missing
From frame.

Please Don't Ever Call Me (Day 397)

When I hear your voice
It's a euphoric trip like no other,
It's as if God has finally called me home.
With every sound you make
I can feel the lightness of your body.
All you produce is harmonious and alluring
But I guess that's the problem and why,
I still love you.

"Where Did The Old You Go?"

Hell, most likely
I mean that *is* where you last
Told him to go, and you know
How obedient he is.

Library

How many times
Will we learn to say goodbye?
It never gets any easier.
You just make it worse
For when you inevitably
Pull me back in.

You'll make it seem so
Ready for me,
So inviting,
Gaping.
I'll be manipulated
Into believing this
Is the gospel.
That the heavens
Have finally touched me,
When really it's just you
Playing with your lovely toy.

You'll lock my arms
And drag me close.
We'll swap tastes through our breaths
As we move around the stage.
Once we've finished this suicide dance

It'll be time to part ways...
Until next time my sweet.
Take care of yourself.

~Learn to disappear for good.

Broken Bones

Sticks and stones
Are just placeholders for
Love and hate
Which are just placeholders for
You.

The Paparazzi

"We're so alike."

"You guys are perfect for each other."

"You two are so cute!"

"You're the best."

"I like that too!"

"I'm sure it'd be amazing."

~What's the issue?

Bermuda

Have you seen him
Since I left?
What does he say to you?
More lies I assume
Yet you're always trying
For him.
What does he say about me?
Huh,
Like you'd ever tell me.

You Always Were

My sweet little princess
Has got up and left me.
My sweet little princess
Does not want to be saved.
My sweet little princess
Takes life with a touch.
My sweet little princess
Stole mine with her blood.

My sweet little princess
Has got up and left me.
My sweet little princess
Has long past forgotten.
My sweet little princess
Thinks not of me.
My sweet little princess
Moved on from her suitor.

Cuneiform

Our messages are
The remnants of
A time lost long ago.

Wonderland

I wonder if you ever think about me in the
afternoons.
I wonder if I ever cross that beautiful mind of
yours.
I wonder if you've missed me the slightest bit.
I wonder if we'll ever see each other again.
I wonder if you'll ever give me that
Second chance in this *God forsaken world.*

Half A Heart

Pull me close
Just to push me far,
Say my name
Then leave a scar,
You want me back
But that's a lie
"Time will tell"
Is your alibi.

Cruel To Be Kind

Help me to understand,
Why you only seem to make
Decisions that change your life
For the worse and not the better.

Damnatio Memoriae

They preach to us that
Love is bound in all things.
That love is the, quote,
Essential identity of life.
So naturally if you will it to
Eradicate all being,
Given the pretenses,
It shall be so and more.

Tendrils of Jealously

The girl of your dreams
Will find a better man.
How could you ever say
You're happy for them?

Time Flies When You're Having Fun

You look so much older than you did
When I first fell in love with you.
I guess that's what hatred does to a person.

Nobody I

I'm your nobody.
I have no perks
Or advantages.
I'm not attractive
Or charming.
I'm only your nobody.
All I possess is
An infinite amount
Of servitude to the one
Whom I love with
My little grey heart.

Nobody II

You're so much more
Than a nobody can be.
You've got enough elegance
And grace to rule the world
For ten millennia.
You're a prism of color
With gold highlights.
A goddess with divine
Power and intellect.
The single molecular force
That drives all the reactions
In my heart.

A nobody's withheld this power.
A nobody has no grace.
You're so much more
Than a nobody can be.
For a deity
The world is yours if
You want it,
And I'm sure you'll
Take it all.

I'd Give Up Everything For You.

Your mind is too constrained,
You could never comprehend
All the ways I dream us to life.

Words Of Encouragement

You can't do it.
You can't.
You just can't do it.
You never could and you never will.
What makes you think this time will be any
different?
So say it with me...
You can't do it.

Verified Account

I must have photographic memory.
I can't erase you
And you know what they say,
Pictures last longer.

Toxicologist

I don't know why
You think
Someone who often
Makes you so angry
So insecure
And so upset
Can somehow
Make you the happiest.

Inputs And Outputs

When you said "I had a great time with you,"
I wish you'd meant it.
The same goes for when
You called me the best ever
Or told me to never change
Because you knew I never could.
I guess you also lied when you told me to
"live a little."

Resurrection

It's all around me, it's on the walls
Across the ocean her lover calls
The vice grip tightens, hear him shout
He will die without a doubt

Look what she's done, see who she is
Taking up everything he thought was his
When he came back, it was too late
Everyone he loved suffered the same fate.

Strawberry Banana

This taste too good to be true.
They way we are...
It could never work itself out
Yet you blow up my phone
And drag me back
Into your kingdom full
Of smiles and hearts
And for what?
Do you feel it
Or are we playing the same
Game of ring around the rosie?

What I've learned is to
Sip it down,
Too much too fast
Can kill.

Pure, Unadulterated, 24 Karat Gold.

It taste rich and lively
Like honey made
From the nectar of
A thousands bees
Sustaining yet plucking
Your beautiful flower.

Vampiric Daydreams

I gave you everything
I could possibly give.
Laid out my beating heart
In front of you.
I'm sure it tasted so sweet.

Succubus

The most important thing
Is to remember who you are
Not what you did.

~Break the coma.

36.5323° N, 116.9325° W

The way you liquified
My youth and sucked
That sweet blood
Straight from the well
That was dying of thirst.

Combustion

All the tears I've shed under your name
Flow less like water, burn more like flame.
What I wouldn't give to be free from this sorrow
It doesn't matter, I'll still feel you tomorrow.
I'll feel you tomorrow and evermore
I'll cry the tears till I'm feeling sore.
When my earth is dry and still in pain
Through all the tears I've shed under your name
I'll pray in silence for your hallowed rain
Which flows less like water, burns more like flame.

Cherry Rocking Chairs

I'd lay in bed and imagine
All the ways we'd grow
Old together,
All the ways we'd live
A full life,
All the ways I could
Make you happy,
Proud,
Even speechless.

We were so young.
We are still young.
It could happen...

With someone else.

Everything Else Is Variable

If there's one
Constant in this world
It's that me and you
Will simply never be together.

~How ever much we dream.

Also check out these books by the same author:

Quadrantaria.

Midnight Milkshakes

Made in the USA
Middletown, DE
29 December 2020